PURPOSE IN MY PAIN

PURPOSE IN MY PAIN

A husband's journey of love, affliction, healing, and restoration.

Dominic C. Reid

Warren, Michigan
Printed in the United States of America

Purpose in my Pain

A husband's journey of love, affliction, healing, and restoration.

Copyright © 2022 Dominic C. Reid

All Rights Reserved

Published in 2022 by Tucker Publishing House, LLC

www.tuckerpublishinghouse.com

Paperback ISBN: 978-1-7377140-8-8

Library of Congress Number: 2022903095

Scriptures cited in this book unless noted are from the KJV and used with permission

Scriptures marked NLT are taken from the HOLY BIBLE, NEW LIVING TRANSLATION

(NLT): Scriptures taken from the HOLY BIBLE, NEW LIVING TRANSLATION, Copyright©

1996, 2004, 2007 by Tyndale House Foundation. Used by permission of Tyndale House

Publishers, Inc., Carol Stream, Illinois 60188. All rights reserved. Used by permission.

Scriptures marked NIV are taken from the NEW INTERNATIONAL VERSION (NIV):

Scripture taken from THE HOLY BIBLE, NEW INTERNATIONAL VERSION ®. Copyright©

1973, 1978, 1984, 2011 by Biblica, Inc.™. Used by permission of Zondervan

Scriptures marked NKJV are taken from the NEW KING JAMES VERSION (NKJV): Scripture

taken from the NEW KING JAMES VERSION®. Copyright© 1982 by Thomas Nelson, Inc.

Used by permission. All rights reserved.

Table Of Contents

Dedication	vii
Foreword	ix
Introduction	xiii
Chapter 1: My Foundation	1
Chapter 2: Falling In Love	6
Chapter 3: Cord Of Three Strands	16
Chapter 4: Discovery Of Infidelity	24
Chapter 5: When The Enemy Attacks	42
Chapter 6: Peace In The Midst Of The Storm	51
Chapter 7: Broken But I'm Healed	64
Chapter 8: Letting Go	77
Chapter 9: Moving Forward	88
About the Author	99

Dedication

I dedicate this book to my Lord and Savior, Jesus Christ. Thank you for giving me the vision and strength to share my testimony with the world. I pray that you get all the glory and honor due to your name.

To my three children, Mariya, Mason, and Jayce, whom I love with all my heart: Keep the Lord first in your lives and work hard at everything you do. Strive for greatness and never give up on pursuing your goals. No matter what obstacles come your way, always trust in God.

To my parents, brothers, and sister who always have my back and love me unconditionally: I'm proud to be part of this family, and I thank you for always being there. I love you all!

To all my other family members and friends who have supported me, I appreciate you all.

To my hometown, the city of Albion!

Foreword

"**Purpose In My Pain**" draws inspiration from the heartbreak Prophet Hosea experienced at the hand of his unfaithful wife. Like Prophet Hosea, Dominic Reid takes us on the riveting journey of his actual life experience of infidelity, heartbreak, and triumph. Historically, adultery was a great social wrong and an assault against the honor and value of the victim. Although contemporary society has relaxed its views regarding the morality of an extramarital affair, the wounded children of divorced parents, poverty, and the fractured souls of both victim and adulterer are evidence of its evil nature. There are thousands of men across the world who have been incarcerated for taking their spouse's life or the life of the offending person in some attempt to avenge the betrayal and dishonor associated with this act. Even the Bible states, "For the woman's jealous husband will be furious, and he will show no mercy when he takes revenge. He will accept no compensation, nor be satisfied with a payoff of any size." (Proverbs 6:34-35) Of course, I am not advocating this type of violence as a response. I am only highlighting the gamut of emotions, rage, and damage that this act can produce in a victim. Adultery is the most common reason cited for divorce. By God's grace, some couples have managed to fight their way back from the brokenness and distrust caused by this selfish act. Countless others find the distrust and broken covenant too great of a divide to cross and choose the way of divorce. In this book, Dominic gives us a relevant, fresh look at the pain of betrayal and the steps he took to discover purpose in the midst thereof. The many things he did to preserve his marriage were noble - almost unbelievable. The depth of the pain he overcame is nothing short of courageous. His transparency will provoke a wide range of emotions, from sympathy to satisfaction and anger to inspiration. His life and his painful story testify of hope and ultimate triumph.

- Hugh Daniel Smith

Introduction

I'm not a famous celebrity whose life is on full display through the media; I am just a regular guy with a story that many people can relate to. Regardless of the status of your relationship, being cheated on hurts, and it hurts deeply. Everyone reacts to hurt and pain differently, you can either allow that hurt and pain to lead you down a destructive path, or you can find purpose in the situation you are going through to lead you on a new path. When a couple decides to get married and make their commitment before God, those vows are sacred and intended to be honored. When those vows are broken, it can cause major repercussions in the relationship. The only way I knew to get through it was with Jesus. With Jesus being my rock and foundation, I was not only able to get through it, but I came out of it a better man. A man tested in his faith, relationship in Christ, and perseverance. I hope my book can inspire couples to not give up on their relationships so easily. I want them to be willing to put in the work and commitment to make a relationship last and trust in the Lord with every aspect of their lives. I hope my book inspires individuals thinking about getting married to ensure they are doing it for the right reasons—and ready for the commitment to being married.

For those of you unfamiliar with the story of Hosea, it is about a prophet in Israel whose name means "he helps." This name likely references his position as a light of hope to those who would repent and turn to God because of his message. Following the command of God, Hosea married Gomer, a bride God described as "a wife of harlotry." Even though my marriage is not exactly like Hosea's, there are some similarities I can relate to. She was not a wife of harlotry, but the Lord did command me to marry her. Hosea's message is closely related to his personal life. The cycle of repentance, redemption, and restoration evident in Hosea's prophecy and his marriage remains intimately connected to our lives. This sequence plays itself out in the lives of real people, reminding us that the Scriptures are far from a mere collection of stories with no relation to real life. I'm one of those real people who can relate to Hosea's story about the pain and struggles as a husband to an unfaithful wife.

God calls His people to do things the opposite of what culture considers popular or desirable. To follow God requires humility to trust that His ways are best. Often, God will not reveal everything to us because He knows we may not want to be obedient and follow His plan. I heard from the Lord to marry her even though He knew everything we would go through. *Why? What was the purpose?* These are the questions I would ask myself over and over again. *What could I have done differently?* The phrases, "God won't put more on us than we can bear," and "God gives

His strongest challenges to His strongest people," rings true in my life.

While we were dating, I remember explaining to her that I would never stay with her if she cheated on me. Adultery is the one action in my marriage I cannot forgive. I would have never imagined that the one thing I said I would never forgive ended up being the obstacle that pushed me into my destiny. Come with me on this journey of love, affliction, healing, and restoration.

CHAPTER ONE

My Foundation

"For I know the plans I have for you," declares the Lord, "plans to prosper you and not to harm you, plans to give you hope and a future."
Jeremiah 29:11 (NIV)

Growing up, I knew I wanted to get married and start a family one day. My parents, who have been married for 44 years, played a significant role in shaping my desire and belief in marriage. I always thought it was so amazing to be with one person for so long and build a life and family together. My parents showed me the amount of effort it takes to have a healthy marriage. They also showed me that it would take time and dedication to succeed at marriage. Although my parents instilled in my siblings and me the do's and don'ts of being married, my dad, in particular, showed me what it's like to be a great dad and husband. The key core principles that my dad shared with me are: to always protect and provide for your family at all times, keep your family covered in prayer, never hit a woman, don't get in the habit of leaving the house when we argue, and to always keep the lines of communication open. These lessons that my dad instilled in me, his words of wisdom and counsel, would mold and shape me into becoming the man I am today. I thank God that I have this type of example of a man in my life.

Even though I received great parenting, the core principles I learned didn't always stick with me. Sometimes when we are young and ignorant, we can drift away from the lessons we were taught. I can count on one hand how many serious relationships I've had. I have always tried to learn from my previous relationships' mistakes. Whether it was not being a good listener, inconsistent communication skills, not showing women I cared enough about them, not spending enough quality time, or just the little things that go a long way in keeping the relationship strong. When I was younger and immature in my thinking and behavior, I developed a lot of selfish characteristics that destroyed relationships and hurt the women I was involved with. I did not like being this way, so I prayed that God would work on my heart to be a better man in my future relationship. I desired to be a man after God's own heart and live up to the example my dad set for me.

My view on marriage was only what I was able to see from my parents. I never knew that one-day marriage for me would be one of the hardest struggles I've ever had. Before I got married, I prayed and asked GOD to send me a woman who was specifically designed for me. I wondered if I had been specific enough, if I should have made a list of qualities, characteristics, and attributes that I desired in a relationship. Although a list may appear to be impractical, I believe we can all agree that having a standard when dating is more vital. Having a standard allows you to be clear about what you want and what you are not ready to tolerate. However, if you are anything like me, a man who takes pride in being patient and seeing the greater good in everyone, some of the standards that I acquired as I developed in my walk with Christ allowed me to meet the woman I previously called my wife.

Falling In Love

CHAPTER TWO

*"Above all, love each
other deeply because love
covers over a multitude of sins."
1 Peter 4:8 (NIV)*

As I grew in my faith, I learned to pray about every big decision in my life, and marriage was no different. My inner peace is my compass in deciding when to move forward. One of the scriptures I meditate on often is Proverbs 3:5-6 (NKJV), which states, "Trust in the Lord with all your heart and lean not on your own understanding; In all your ways, acknowledge Him, and He shall direct your paths." That was the process I used before I decided to get married. With the help of GOD and the advice from men in my family that church was the perfect place to find a good wife, I began my journey in 2012.

When I moved from Albion to Metro Detroit, I was excited about my new job as a school counselor. I was looking forward to all the opportunities in store for me personally and professionally. Meeting a woman in the church seems ideal because one can assume that ladies at church have a relationship with the Lord, mature, willing to be led by a God-fearing man, and desire to be a great wife. Although those statements may be accurate, women in the church, just like any other woman, are not exempt from having deep-rooted issues that need to be healed. At the end of the day, we all have issues that need to be addressed. If those issues are not addressed appropriately, they will manifest in our relationship.

I remember when I joined my new church, I felt like I was ready to meet someone, and as fate would have it, I was approached by a young woman, and for some reason, our connection felt right. She was so beautiful and had the prettiest smile I had ever seen. I was intrigued by her beauty, but it took a long time before I pursued her because she had a daughter, which gave me a reason to pause. I always had reservations about getting too seriously involved with a woman who had kids, so just because she was beautiful, that would not be a good enough reason. I heard stories from other guys I know about how much drama can involve raising somebody else's child. More so, if the parents don't get along, and I wanted no parts of it. However, week after week, I would see her and become more curious about getting to know her. I thought to myself *should I loosen up on my standards and not be dead set against dating a woman who has kids and give it a try?* Having the opportunity to raise a child that isn't my biological daughter has been one of the greatest blessings of my life. I'm glad I loosened up on that standard and decided to take a chance.

We dated for two years; in the beginning, things were amazing. Whether it was having picnics, going to the Tigers game, going to comedy shows, plays, hanging out at each other's homes, road trips out of town, etc. She was easy to talk to, and she had a great personality and a very infectious laugh. We would talk on the phone for hours, just getting to know one another. My parents loved her, she got along well with my siblings, and all my other family members and friends thought highly of her as well. Our time together was going well, and it felt like we were building something special. This stage of a relationship is usually the "honeymoon" stage. We can see all the best qualities in a person, and the true colors don't usually reveal themselves. This is also the stage where we see the representation of what people only want us to see. It is imperative we take our time and get to know the person on a deep level. I truly believe building a foundation of a relationship on a solid friendship first is key to having a successful relationship. As my elders would say, look deep before you leap. Beyond just the physical attraction, really get to know their heart and their emotional, mental, and spiritual stability. The good characteristics can be overshadowed by childhood hurt, past trauma, and the setting of healthy boundaries. These are the issues we tend not to discuss in the early stages of relationships because of fear, judgment, or rejection, but in order to have a healthy relationship discussing your past with your partner is extremely important. We may not divulge everything in the earlier part of the relationship, but before any type of long-term commitment takes place, these issues should be discussed.

I vividly remember there was a time I went to see her, she was lying in bed, and she seemed very down and depressed. As we talked, she started explaining how she wasn't unhappy with us but other areas of her life. However, she did state that maybe we should 'take a break' in our relationship. I had no desire to give up on her or us. I wanted to show her that I cared about her and she was worth fighting for. I encouraged her to take all the time she needed and not make a rushed decision, and after a few days, if she still felt like we should take a break, then I would accept it. Could this have been a warning sign that I did not pay enough attention to? Was she trying to tell me something without saying much? Out of fear she would be making a mistake or that I would find somebody else, she decided to stay in the relationship when in reality, she was having doubts. All of those doubts, fears, and uncertainties would show up in a destructive way later in our relationship.

In October 2013, I went on a spiritual kairos retreat for three days. At this retreat center, there were no televisions, and I was not allowed to use my phone. There were no distractions and plenty of opportunities to pray and spend time listening to the voice of God. At this retreat, I discovered that I could hear God a lot clearer when I turned off the television and spent quiet time in His presence. I heard from God clear as day that she was the woman I was supposed to marry. The voice was so clear that it felt like someone was in the room talking to me.

Even though she was young and had a child, she was the woman I was supposed to make my wife. I also heard God say I would be the balancer in both of their lives. I would be everything she needed in a husband but not everything she wanted. The relationship would not be perfect, and we would go through many trials. It takes a village to raise a child, and I would need to fill in the gaps and help make sure everything is complete. When it came to her daughter, the message was that everything is not about me and how I envision my family. This sweet little girl will need me in her life as well to help her grow spiritually and get to know the Lord.

Once I finished hearing from God, I was at peace and content with spending the rest of my life with her. I knew as long as we kept the Lord first in our marriage, we would make it and could overcome anything. I learned throughout my marriage that being obedient is not always easy, but there are many rewards and blessings for being obedient to God. He is a faithful God! I feel like I did everything right when it came time to find my future wife. I prayed about it and was patient. I heard from God and was obedient in what he told me to do. Even though God tells us to do something doesn't mean we won't face trials and tribulations along the way. Our faith is often being tested to see if we really trust God and help us grow spiritually. James 1:2-3 (NLT) says, "When troubles of any kind come your way, consider it an opportunity for great joy. For you know that when your faith is tested, your endurance has a chance to grow." It is important to trust in God no matter what we go through because He can help us overcome any situation. As situations were about to arise, this is exactly what I did by putting my trust in God!

CHAPTER THREE

Cord Of Three Strands

*"A cord of three strands is
not quickly broken."
Ecclesiastes 4:12 (NIV)*

A husband and wife connected to God is the representation of the Cord of three strands. It represents the joining of one man and one woman with God into a marriage relationship. For a marriage to be successful, it takes all three, and God must always be at its center. As long as those strands are connected, nothing or nobody can separate the union. I knew for my marriage to be what it was intended to be, God had to be our rock and foundation. "The man who finds a wife finds a treasure, and he receives favor from the Lord." (Proverbs 18:22 NLT)

I recommend that any couple who plans to get married go through premarital counseling. It is well worth it and very beneficial. According to statistics, only 44% of couples who get married today agree to premarital counseling before taking their vows. During premarital counseling, have discussions on marriage expectations and role beliefs, how the past affects our future (this is the area where we should have put more emphasis), resolving future conflicts, and so much more. Our spiritual advisor had us go through many exercises and assignments to ensure we were ready to be married. He asked all the right questions, but one analogy he made about marriage still stands out in my mind until this day. He stated that marriage is like a farmer purchasing a piece of land. Owning a piece of land requires much responsibility and hard work to blossom, just like marriage takes much effort for it to be fruitful. You have to work the land, plant seeds, dig up weeds, and continue to put work into the ground, so it's beneficial and prosperous.

In your marriage, you will have to:

- pull up weeds (the weeds are the issues we deal with in our marriage)
- work the land (spend quality time together, communicate, etc.)
- continue to date one another (so it's fruitful)

- sacrifice for one another (so it prospers)

He asked me, is she worth the purchase? That was a powerful question knowing what I know now. I do not regret marrying her. I learned a long time ago that there is no progress without struggle. Everything in life won't always be easy, so you have to be willing to fight for the things worth fighting for. I believed this marriage was worth fighting for. When issues arise within our marriages, it takes two people to make it work. If there is a half commitment from either spouse, the marriage will not survive. Solid communication is a key ingredient to a successful marriage. There should be no fear in a healthy marriage. If the relationship is strong and solid, then there is nothing you shouldn't be able to communicate to your spouse.

Leading up to our marriage, she did not show any signs or communicate that something was bothering her. She would work, help plan the wedding, and still be an attentive mother and fiance'. She hid her infidelity well during this time. I don't know if it was because we weren't married yet, so maybe she didn't feel guilty or ashamed about it. Deep down, she was struggling, but instead of reaching out for help, she was trying to deal with it independently. The word of God tells us to "Confess your sins to each other and pray for each other so that you may be healed." (James 5:16 NLT) Keeping our sins in the dark only leads to destruction. It may not happen right away, but eventually, everything will come to light, and it will cause devastating effects for everyone involved.

Getting to the root of our issues is important because if not, it will keep showing up in some form of way, either mentally or physically. It's no different from weeds growing in your yard; if you don't pull up the roots and put in some treatment, the weeds will return, and the process continues repeatedly. *Did she decide to marry me for herself or her daughter? Was she rushing into a marriage at such a young age? Did she really want to be married right now?* These were questions that would be raised later once everything came to light. I don't know why I couldn't see anything was wrong during this time. I honestly did not think she would hurt me in this way. I learned to never put anything past anyone, and it's always those closest to you that end up hurting us the most.

I remember the morning of our wedding, I was praying in my bedroom. While I was praying, she came over to our apartment and walked into the room. When I looked up and saw her face, I knew something was wrong. She had the saddest look on her face, and she started crying. She told me the banquet hall where we were supposed to get married in seven hours did not have any power, and they did not have a backup generator. We were both devastated, but I let her know everything would be alright, and we prayed about the situation. The banquet hall owner let us know that if the power was not back by 1 pm, they would move everything down the street to an alternate banquet hall. With no power at 1 pm, our wedding was shifted to the banquet hall down the street. The employees did a great job of redecorating and getting the site together.

The wedding ceremony was beautiful, and we exchanged our vows in front of our family and friends. Before we even got married, I never would have imagined that she had already been cheating on me. It's funny how things can appear one way in life, but they are totally different in reality. I was fully invested in this marriage and this partnership we were building. The foundation of our marriage started with lies and deception. I always wondered if the power going out at the banquet hall was a sign to expect the unexpected and that trouble was coming in this marriage. When the storms came, how was I going to handle it? What would my response be to the issues coming in our marriage? The trials that we may think are too difficult to overcome are designed to help us grow in our faith. It's important to remember anything that comes our way in life; God can see us through it.

Discovery Of Infidelity

"God's will is for you to be holy, so stay away from all sexual sin. Then each of you will control his own body and live in holiness and honor."

1 Thessalonians 4:3-4 (NIV)

CHAPTER FOUR

Many couples deal with adultery regularly in their marriages. Statistics show the overall numbers are extremely high. According to the Journal of Marriage and Divorce, 70 percent of married American couples cheat at least once in their marriage. Some would ask why the numbers are so high and what causes people to cheat. According to the best-selling author, Mark Manson, the main two reasons people cheat are because of an oversized need for self-gratification and the lack of real intimacy. Manson states, "Self gratifying cheaters are constantly focused on their own gratification because they feel so miserable about themselves that they need to make themselves feel good to cover it up all the time." How she felt about herself caused her not to value herself or our marriage. Her lustful and selfish behaviors outweighed her desire to be a loyal and respectful wife.

I realized something was off with her, but I just did not realize adultery was part of the equation. She had never given me a reason to mistrust her, and she did a good job of keeping all of her skeletons in the closet. When we live double lives, it can begin to take a toll on us in a lot of ways. I guess this was one of the things that stood out, and it was like dealing with two different women. Some days I couldn't recognize who she was based on her behaviors. I thought to myself, who is this woman? Where is the woman I fell in love with? In reality, she was the same woman I fell in love with. I believe it is important to be healed from any past issues before entering a marriage. If you are not fully healed, you will bring those problems into your marriage. You have to truly know who you are before even considering building a life with someone else.

I noticed little subtle changes in her, like the reluctance to pray together and do our marriage devotionals. Sometimes it was like pulling teeth for her to do this with me. I understand that prayer in a marriage is very important, so I wanted us to set aside time to pray together daily. As the head of the household, I felt this was one of my responsibilities to lead us in this process, and I took it very seriously. The resistance to us building together through prayer and devotion was troubling. I knew our marriage was under spiritual attack. The enemy was out to destroy not only the marriage but for me in the process. When the enemy attacks, you have to be willing to fight back, don't just sit back and allow him to destroy your life. We have to learn how to speak the word of God over our lives and stop believing the lies of the enemy. Always remember the enemy has no power or authority over us. We have everything we need inside of us to defeat the enemy. Surrounding ourselves with other believers is always a good place to start, so we attended a two-day marriage retreat. When we first signed up, she was excited about it, but she tried to find reasons not to attend as the date got closer. She was adamant about attending this party her co-workers invited her to instead. However, we came to a compromise, and we ended up attending the retreat and then the party afterward.

On the first night of the retreat, we did a few activities, and she was not feeling it. Her body language and facial expressions showed that she did not want to be there. As we finished the first night of the retreat, we headed home. As she was getting ready to attend the party, I told her I wanted to come with her to the party, and she became irritated.

She made me feel like crap at this point, so I did not want to go with her anymore. I stayed home that night, but deep in my gut, I knew she was up to no good. She left for the party and ended up coming home at 3 am. I checked my phone to see if she sent a text or called, neither to both. I pretended like I was asleep as she moved quietly and gently across the room, trying not to wake me up. I watched her with a squinted eye as she tried to slither in bed like a snake.

I let her get comfortable for about a minute before I popped up and asked why she was getting into the apartment at 3 am. She lied and told me she didn't just get home. She said she lost track of time because she got something to eat after the party. *Really*? I didn't believe that and felt there was more to it. I knew she was lying, but I was sitting there trying to process everything. I continued to press and asked why she didn't at least call or text? She said she was not thinking and that she was sorry.

After our conversation, she got up and went to take a shower. As I was lying in bed listening to the shower running, I immediately got angry. I went into the bathroom and asked her why she was taking another shower. She said she could smell the cigarettes on her clothes. Another story I didn't believe, so I asked her point-blank if she was cheating on me.

She looked me dead in my eyes and said, "No."

In my heart, I knew the answer was yes; all the signs from this evening revealed she was cheating, but I just couldn't bring myself to believe it. I didn't have any concrete proof, but things were about to change rapidly.

On the morning of day two of the retreat, she had a defeated and tired look in her eyes. I asked her what was wrong, and she shed a tear, "I'm just tired." Was she physically tired? Spiritually tired? Emotionally tired? Mentally tired? Was she tired of cheating on me and pretending like everything was ok? I believe it was a combination of everything. I think the guilt had finally eaten away at her, and she could no longer take it.

What do you do when you finally reach your breaking point in life? Do you continue down the same dark path of destruction, or do you turn to Jesus, the one who can bring you out of darkness and turn your life completely around? Jesus said, "Come unto me all you who are weary and burdened, and I will give you rest." Matthew 11:28. (NIV) Once we arrived at the retreat for day two, she spoke privately to some of the other married couples. I sat on the bench in the lobby as she spoke to them. I had no idea what they could've been talking about, but I felt uneasy in my spirit. When they came out of the room, my spiritual advisor pulled me into a private area and asked me if I still loved her? I told him yes.

He asked me, "Do you think you can be there for her no matter what she tells you?"

"Yes."

He asked, "Is this land still worth the purchase?"

"Yes."

When I think about this now, it reminds me of Jesus asking Peter three times if he loves

Him in John 21:15-18. Three times I was asked if I loved her because he knew our love and marriage were about to be tested. He told me not to ask her questions about their conversation or try to resolve anything before we met as a group on Tuesday.

As soon as we got in the car, I asked her if she had cheated on me. This is exactly what I was told *not* to do; I couldn't help it because my anxiety was so high. She deflected the question and didn't deny it. At that point, it was even more confirmed in my heart that adultery had taken place in our marriage. Compared to this morning, she looked more relieved, like she had just gotten a huge weight off her chest. The sins we commit can weigh us down if we don't get that stuff off our chest. God's grace and mercy are so wonderful that we can still come to him when we make bad choices. The word of God tells us, "…..Let us strip off every weight that slows us down, especially the sin that so easily trips us up." (Hebrews 12:1 NLT)

I was so anxious and nervous waiting for Tuesday to come so we could talk about this. Those were the longest three days of my life, and I could barely eat or sleep. Anyone who knows me understands I love to eat, so when it's hard for me to eat, trust me, I'm going through it. I stayed consistent in prayer for the next 3 days for the Lord to cover me during our meeting. Tuesday was finally here, and the drive to the meeting was quiet between us. I was processing what she would tell me, and I could only imagine what she thought and felt during the drive.

Once we arrived, my heart began to race immediately because I knew I was about to hear the words I said I would never forgive her for. When she turned towards me and said she had been cheating on me before we even got married, my heart sank to the bottom of my stomach. I sat there quietly with my right leg crossed over my left knee and my left index finger on the left side of my head with my thumb on my face. I was feeling so much anger, confusion, and pain. I didn't understand how we had gotten to this place in our relationship/marriage. I wasn't sure if I wanted to stay married to her anymore. Our spiritual team thought the marriage was salvageable because they never met a man who handled that type of news so calmly and relaxed in all their years of ministry. It frightened them that I was so calm, and I scared myself because I was unsure how I would react once we were alone.

The ride home was quiet; I felt the anger in the pit of my stomach like the size of a bowling ball, and my heart felt like it had a hole in it. Her betrayal crushed my heart, and it took so long to get the thoughts of her being with other men out of my mind. She expressed remorse, said she was sorry, and wouldn't do it again. She poured her heart out to me and asked me to please forgive her. I remember feeling an overwhelming sense of compassion, forgiveness, and love towards her. I knew the spirit of the Lord was with me because deep down in my mind, I wanted to choke the life out of her. But instead, I pulled her in for a hug and kissed her on the forehead. I wanted to forgive her, but this was easier said than done.

The next few days, I could cut the tension with a knife. I barely said a word to her, and the sheer sight of her face would put me in a bad mood. I knew I couldn't go on living like this because it wasn't healthy for me. I was extremely short with my stepdaughter. I was not proud of that because she was innocent in all of this and did not know what was going on. However, she could tell something was wrong by my body language and lack of communication.

I was so full of rage and anger, so one night, as my ex-wife slept, I got out of bed, went to the kitchen, and got a knife. I had all types of thoughts racing through my mind, and I truly contemplated stabbing or slitting her throat. I thought about the impact this would have on my stepdaughter and the entire family if I were to kill her.

When I had moments like that, I would always call on the name of the Lord, and my anger would cease. The word of God tells us to "Refrain from anger and turn from wrath; do not fret, it leads only to evil." (Psalm 37:8 NIV) It's ok to struggle and be in pain, but continue to lean on God in those moments of heartbreak and pain. Find the strength to push forward and trust Him in the process. I do not know where I would be if I didn't have a relationship with Jesus and have a foundation in prayer and reading the bible.

My life was in shambles, and it was only about to get worse. One night we were watching t.v. and her phone kept beeping as she was receiving messages. I asked her who she was texting, and she replied that it was a co-worker about work stuff. When she went into the kitchen, I checked her phone because, at this point, I didn't believe a word that came out of her mouth. She neglected to mention it was a male co-worker, and they were not talking about work. When she returned to the couch, I asked her if she was still cheating on me. She sat there quietly, looking straight forward, then turned towards me and said yes. It had only been a short time when she said she was sorry and wouldn't cheat again, but she returned to the same behaviors. Not only that, but she had the audacity to be sitting next to me texting another man. That made me feel lower than low like this woman really doesn't care about my feelings or respect me at all. I was angry even more because now I felt like she was taking me for a joke and really disrespecting me.

As we talked about everything that happened before and during our marriage, I was extremely disturbed. My intensity towards her got so heated that I kicked her out of the apartment, along with my stepdaughter, and told her not to come back. Looking back on it now, that was wrong on my part. Instead of kicking them out, I should have just left. I knew she could go to her parent's house and stay there, which was important to me even under the circumstances. We often do things out of anger that we regret; we don't know how our actions will impact others. The way I treated her that night frightened and hurt her. I always reflect on the phrase, "hurt people hurt other people." Adultery would cause a 7-year marriage to slowly deteriorate, and things would never be the same between us again.

The best way to describe my world during this time was being planted and deeply rooted in the middle of a tornado. I could feel and see my world crumbling all around me, but I wouldn't be broken completely. I was about to go through one of the toughest battles in my life but looking back on it now, God had built me up for this moment. The power of the Holy Spirit had a hold on me, and it wouldn't let me go. Jeremiah 17:7 (NIV) says, "But blessed is the one who trusts in the Lord, whose confidence is in him." When I say the Lord was my rock, I cannot stress that enough. Even when I was at my weakest moments physically, I still felt strong *spiritually*. This was just another affirmation in my life that **Jesus is real.**

When The Enemy Attacks

"For we are not fighting against flesh-and-blood enemies, but against evil rulers and authorities of the unseen world, against mighty powers in this dark world, and against evil spirits in the heavenly places."

Ephesians 6:12 (NLT)

My world had been turned upside down. I was depleted. I was numb. I felt defeated. I was not myself. It felt like the enemy had stolen everything from me in a blink of an eye. It is important to recognize who your enemy really is. She was not my enemy, but the devil and his forces were my real enemy. He is the one who was trying to destroy my family and me. You have to recognize his schemes and tactics and rely on the power of God in order to defeat him. If he can entice one spouse to find pleasure anywhere else, then he has succeeded. His ultimate goal was to destroy our relationship with Christ and ultimately each other. The resistance of us praying together and doing our devotions was a sign we were not on the same page spiritually. We are not all in the same place in our relationship with Christ. This process is a journey for all of us. In any marriage, there may be a situation where one spouse is more conscious spiritually than the other. However, that is ok as long as the spouse who is not more conscious is willing to do the necessary things to grow spiritually. In my case, she was not willing to grow with me and was more consumed with worldly things. The enemy had been given a foothold in our marriage, and he was about to take full advantage of it.

Our marriage had just been hit with a major blow, and we were no longer living in the same place. One of the enemy's tricks is to isolate us from other people. He knows if he can get us alone in our thoughts and feelings, it is easier to attack us. The next time I saw her, she looked mentally and physically exhausted. She had gotten to a place where she didn't understand her worth or purpose anymore. To witness someone I loved struggling so much hurt me deeply. She told me repeatedly I deserved someone better than her, and she wasn't worthy of being my wife. I could tell by how she was talking that the enemy had been attacking her mind. I disagreed and let her know everyone makes mistakes, which didn't have to define who she is as a person or a wife.

One of the best books I've ever read was The Battlefield of the Mind by Joyce Myers. She felt unworthy, guilty, ashamed, confused; all of these are tools the devil will use to keep us in a defeated state of mind. He knows if he can attack our minds, negative behaviors will soon follow. Battles are often won and lost in our minds with our own thinking. Isaiah 26:3 (NLT) says, "You will keep in perfect peace all who trust in you, all whose thoughts are fixed on you!" It is important to know when we are in the midst of a battle to keep our minds on Jesus. If we allow our minds to focus on our problems and circumstances, it can weigh us down. It is also important not to believe the lies of the devil. Once we are vulnerable, it's easy to believe those lies and allow doubt to creep in. We have to know who God says we are and His promises for us.

I recognized we were in a major crisis, so I did everything to encourage and help uplift her. She was crying uncontrollably at this point and decided to get out of the car in the middle of our conversation. She took off running down the street, and I chased her right behind her to calm her down and get her back in the car. I grabbed hold of her and got her out of the street. I didn't let her go until I could get her back in the car. I let her know we could go home and finish talking, and she was ok with that. Once I started driving, there was a weird shift in the atmosphere. It felt like something else had taken hold of her. She started scratching her face and forearms uncontrollably, really hard and making weird noises in a strange tone. She grabbed hold of the door handle and tried to unlock the door to jump out. I will never forget this night as long as I live; this was literally like a scene out of a movie. I couldn't believe what was happening because I had never witnessed anything like this in my life. The entire time while all this was happening, I was just calling on the name of Jesus. There will be or have been moments in our life when we may be at a loss for words or don't even know what to pray in moments of a crisis. Call on the name of Jesus, and everything will be alright. There is deliverance, power, and victory in the name of Jesus. She got frustrated as I continued to lock the door as she was trying to unlock it. At that point, she grabbed ahold of the steering wheel, and I immediately knocked her hands off the wheel. I became indignant and spoke directly to her, and whatever had taken hold of her with authority.

"You better calm your butt down. You ain't that crazy. Now, if you want to jump out of the moving car, go ahead, but you're not about to kill me in the process." After that, she started crying, and her voice returned to normal, and she said, "Dominic, help me, please." I told her everything would be alright, and we will be home in a minute. At this point, it felt like I was experiencing hell on earth. After what I witnessed that night, I thought, could I really divorce and cut her off at a time like this? I had never seen her like this before, and I knew she needed help. What type of man or husband would I be to not be there for her through this process. I loved her, and I would not turn my back on her, so I knew that night I would fight for her and our marriage. I knew we had a long road ahead of us, but I always felt she was worth it. I was dealing with my own disappointment, hurt, and pain; now, on top of that trying to fix our marriage in the process. As a man, I felt I had a lot on my plate and the weight of the world on my shoulders. I was dealing with a lot emotionally, mentally, physically, and spiritually.

When you love someone, the love does not just go away when they hurt or disappoint you. Unconditional love means just that, to love someone unconditionally, not based on what they can do for you in return. Through all their flaws, through all the mistakes, through all the ups and downs. The same way God loves us unconditionally. The word of God tells us in 1 Corinthians

13:4-8,(NIV) Love is patient, love is kind. It does not envy; it does not boast; it is not proud. It does not dishonor others; it is not self-seeking, it is not easily angered, it keeps no record of wrongs. Love does not delight in evil but rejoices with the truth. It always protects, always trusts, always hope, always perseveres. Love never fails." I hoped that she would realize how much I loved her, and that would help us get back on track in our marriage.

Peace In The Midst Of The Storm

"Now may the Lord of peace himself give you his peace at all times and in every situation...."
2 Thessalonians 3:16 (NLT)

CHAPTER SIX

It was horrible to be in love with someone I could not trust. I took three steps forward and two steps back. The steps forward felt so good, and the steps backward felt so terrible. Processing everything that happened in my marriage and figuring out how to move forward was a grueling process. The pain I felt in my heart was so unbearable some days. My trust in her had been completely broken. By the grace of God, I was able to keep pushing forward every day. I knew I could not make it without Him. I've never been the type of man to wallow in my misery. I was determined to get everything back that was stolen from me. I knew I had a long road of healing and recovery ahead of me, but I intended to make it happen. It's easy to praise God when everything is going well in our lives, but it can be a lot more difficult when everything is not going well.

Often, we want instant gratification to make us feel better when we are hurting. It's a natural reaction to want to numb the pain with sex, drugs, alcohol, or otherworldly things. I've tried some of those things in my past, and it didn't work out well. So I know none of those things can truly heal me. It gave me a false sense of healing and comfort, but I knew I needed true healing deep in my soul. The Lord is the only one who can heal us completely and restore the brokenness inside of us. Psalm 147:3 (NIV) tells us, "He heals the brokenhearted and binds up their wounds." We have to rely on His strength to get us through the difficult times in life.

As I was overcoming everything I had gone through, all the scriptures I had studied started coming back to me. It was like the Holy Spirit was reminding me of what I had learned. I leaned on my foundation in Christ to get my life back in order.

These were the scriptures I laid my faith in during this moment.

"When you pass through the waters, I will be with you, and when you pass through the rivers, they will not sweep over you. When you walk through the fire, you will not be burned; the flames will not set you ablaze."
(Isaiah 43:2 NIV)

"You will keep in perfect peace all who trust in you, all whose thoughts are fixed on you."
(Isaiah 26:3 NLT)

"So do not fear, for I am with you; do not be dismayed, for I am your God. I will strengthen you and help you; I will uphold you with my righteous right hand."
(Isaiah 41:10 NIV)

I read these scriptures every day and meditated deeply to really allow the words to get into my mind and spirit. I buried myself in prayer, praise and worship, and the word of GOD. I knew I had to take my prayer life to another level. I couldn't stay in the same place spiritually and expect to overcome what I was going through. The more life threw at me, the higher I had to go. I poured my heart out to GOD and laid everything at his feet. When I would finish praying, my heart would feel so much lighter, like I had just released so many burdens. I loved the way I felt when I would pray, so I prayed in the morning, at work, and relentlessly when I got home in the evening.

My atmosphere would change from dark and gloomy to joyful and hopeful during my praise and worship moments. Praise and worship strengthened my spirit and gave me the energy to keep going day to day. Reading the word of GOD would touch my mind and give me the wisdom and understanding I needed to remind me daily that as long as I stayed connected to Jesus, everything would be alright. Prayer, praise and worship, and the word of GOD would be my daily routine. Even though I did all this stuff daily, I don't want you to think this was an easy process. I began to notice that during the days I was feeling my lowest, I was not spending enough time in prayer. Sometimes I allowed my flesh to get the best of me, and at times it was difficult to pray, read my bible and worship God. I allowed my feelings and negative thinking to get in the way of my healing process. I would find myself drifting away from the place where strength and peace resided, and that was with Jesus. The more I prayed through, the better I felt and the more peace I had daily. I really had to be specific in my prayers for God to heal my mind. It's important to always evaluate where we are in the healing process and be honest with ourselves. Don't try to rush it; just take it one day at a time. Some days were extremely difficult, but knowing this is part of the process is important. All of my emotions, thoughts, and feelings were normal, and what I was going through was the stages of grief.

When dealing with traumatic situations, grief will come into play. The 7 stages of grief are shock/denial, pain/guilt, anger and bargaining, depression, upward turn, reconstruction/work through, and acceptance/hope. One of the important things to know about these stages is that we may not go through every one of them, and we may not experience them in order. I would bounce between shock/denial and pain/guilt stages. I was mourning the breakdown in our relationship because the truth is our relationship would never be the same again. As the shock began to wear off, I thought if there was anything I could have done differently to prevent this from happening. The truth is I was a good man to her, and there is nothing I could have done to stop her actions. It's a natural reaction to blame ourselves when we get cheated on. We think if we had done this or done more of that, then maybe our spouses would have been faithful to us. However, I realized that I could not blame myself for her selfish actions, and she would do what she wanted to do regardless of how I treated her.

Often, we don't understand the purpose of our pain while we are going through the trials, but as time goes by, we can start to see things differently, and they become much clearer. One of my favorite quotes is "pray hardest when it is hardest to pray." I want to encourage everyone when life gets tough; this is when we really need to seek the Lord the most and not turn away from Him. 1 Chronicles 16:11 (NIV) instructs us to "Look to the Lord and His strength; seek His face always." During the good and bad times in life, seek His face. It is easy to give up and be discouraged when life beats us down. That is what the enemy wants us to do. But we need to push past the pain and speak to the Lord about our feelings. It's ok for us to express those raw emotions to the Lord. He wants to hear our deepest feelings; just lay everything at His feet. The closer I stayed to the Lord, the more my spirit was lifted. I realized

I had the blueprint to fully heal and grow from this experience. That blueprint was the Lord. The Lord can take our worst situations and make something beautiful. Romans 8:28 (NIV) tells us, "And we know that in all things God works for the good of those who love him, who have been called according to His purpose." I believed the Lord would use everything I had been through with her to take me to another level. The enemy thought this would destroy me, but I serve a mighty God, and I refused to let her actions destroy me. I would not allow the enemy to steal my joy and peace; I would not allow him to kill my faith; I would not allow him to destroy my view of marriage. I am more than a conqueror, and I am an overcomer by the blood of the lamb and the word of my testimony.

My support system during this time was unbelievable. During the heavy times in life, we need other people to lean on. As men, we may feel it's "soft" or too embarrassing to ask for help, but God never designed for us to be loners in this world but to connect with other people, especially when we need comfort. 1 Thessalonians 5:11 (NIV) says, "Therefore encourage one another and build each other up, just as in fact you are doing." The church leaders helped me through the entire process, day or night. I truly appreciated their brotherly love. They called me in the mornings on their way to work, and they would call in the evenings on their way home. They would pray with me daily and give me encouraging, uplifting words. Their prayers and words of encouragement helped me out a lot.

I know my family would have been there for me too, but I intentionally didn't tell them what was going on. I felt it would be irresponsible to tell them everything that was going on in my marriage. It was so early in my marriage, and things were up in the air between us. I didn't want her relationship with my family to be ruined. I didn't want the family dynamics to be awkward for anyone. I wanted to preserve that for as long as possible for everyone's sake. It's important to have support when going through trials and tribulations. One of the enemy's tricks is to deceive us into thinking we can get through issues like this on our own. He knows if he can get us alone in our thoughts and feelings, it is easier to attack us. God never intended for us to be alone and isolated from other people. We need other people to survive in this world. We all need to have someone in our corner when life throws us curve balls. I had plenty of alone time to reflect, pray, read and worship. My days were long, and my nights were short. The peace of God was with me every step of the way. There wasn't a day when I didn't experience his peace. I continued to trust in the Lord because I knew He was the only one who could heal me and get me back in the right space mentally.

Broken But I'm Healed

"He gives strength to the weary and increases the power of the weak."
Isaiah 40:29 (NIV)

Over time certain areas of our relationship began to improve. One of the main things we were working on was our communication, so I knew I needed to learn how to express my feelings to her. Good communication and honesty were important as we moved forward in our marriage. I thanked God for the strength he gave me daily.

I would be so lost without him. He has been my rock throughout this entire storm. My life will never be the same (not necessarily in a negative way), and my marriage will never be the same after this. I prayed that God would restore my trust in her because it was not present at the time. I knew this would take some time, but my faith was always in God. I realized there was nothing I could do to change her. I learned a long time ago you cannot change a person's behavior. People have to want to change for themselves to change their behavior. God was the only one who could change her because it was a heart issue. I saw little glimpses of change in her, so I praised God for every moment of growth I saw in her. With God, all things are possible, and I was keeping my faith in God to turn our marriage around.

We had decided to renew our vows and make a fresh start in our marriage one day. She also suggested that we attend marriage counseling, but I did not think we needed it right now. I figured we could continue meeting with our spiritual leaders, praying together, and everything would work out. Looking back on it, we should have definitely attended professional marriage counseling as another tool to help us move forward in our marriage. I think it would have benefited us tremendously. This is probably one of my biggest regrets throughout all of this. Always exhaust all options and do everything possible to make your marriage work. Marriage is not easy, and it takes a lot of work to be successful. Getting married is easy, but staying married can be challenging.

We did not have any children between us at this point in our marriage. We had discussed having kids, and we felt this was the right time for that to happen. Often, when married couples go through problems, they may feel having a baby may help resolve the issues between them, or it could make them worse. I think it was a mixture of both for us. Planning to have a baby was not a mistake, but it was probably poor timing. We should have been more focused on fixing our relationship first and ensuring proper healing was taking place. I truly believe God does not make mistakes, and His plans prevail every time.

Before we renewed our vows, she suffered a miscarriage, and we were both devastated. She wasn't far along but knowing she was pregnant with my first child hurt deeply. I was excited to have my first biological child. I spent many nights mourning her miscarriage and the birth of our child. I never truly forgot that experience. It makes me wonder if the miscarriage pulled us closer together or further apart. I thought this would be just one more thing for us to overcome in our marriage.

After our miscarriage, our spiritual advisor told us something very interesting. He explained in the heavenly realms, we were no longer married. Even though we were legally married on earth, we were no longer married in the spiritual realm. When she committed adultery, the covenant we made before God was broken, and this needed to be made right before we would be blessed with a child. We need to understand God requires things from us before doors will be opened. Hebrews 11:6 (NIV) says, "Without faith, it is impossible to please God because anyone who comes to him must believe that he exists and that he rewards those who earnestly seem." He is a God who requires repentance, obedience, and order. We both took these words to heart, so we renewed our vows on Sunday, August 28th, and within two weeks after renewing our vows, we found out she was pregnant. So the blessing was already given before we decided to renew our vows. God is so faithful, and he knows our hearts. He knows what we are going to do before we even do it.

Even though we had gone through a lot in our first two years of marriage, I believe God was still for us and blessing us along the way. I knew she was the woman I was supposed to marry, which is the main reason I continued to fight for her no matter what. I tried to be a faithful and obedient husband, not only because God told me to, but I was committed to this marriage and her.

We were both excited about the pregnancy and felt this was a fresh start. Having my first child should have been a thrilling experience for me, but this was not always the case. I would still struggle with my emotions towards her at some of the worst times during her pregnancy. Sometimes I was loving, and sometimes I was distant. I would lay my hands on her belly and pray for her and the baby, but mostly I only did this while she was sleeping at night. This annoyed her that I did this; she would always ask me why I did these things while she was asleep. She wanted to experience me talking to the baby and praying for her. I think subconsciously, I had doubts if the baby was really mine. This was hard to admit to her, but I always wondered in the back of my mind. At this point, I still did not trust her, and honestly, I don't know if I ever did for the rest of our marriage. I allowed that trust factor to drive me crazy to the point I wasn't always there for her during this pregnancy like I should've been. This was another one of my regrets during our marriage. However, I learned not to beat myself up so much when I was having my down days and just continued to lean on God. I found renewed strength when I realized my inner healing was still happening even during the bad days. No matter how I was feeling, my mindset was to keep moving forward with God.

Considering this was my first child, I should have made this an incredible experience for us. If we allow negative thoughts to fester in our minds, it can cause us to do and say things we may regret. God was doing amazing things in our marriage, and the enemy wanted to destroy it. John 10:10 (NKJV) tells us, "The thief does not come except to steal, and to kill, and to destroy. I have come that they may have life and that they may have it more abundantly." The thief will try to find a way to steal, kill or destroy your marriage, relationships, family, peace, future, happiness, joy, goals, and purpose. I understood that everything I would have to overcome would be mental at this point. Asking God to heal my mind was included in my daily prayers. I do not know where I would be if I did not have a foundation and relationship with Jesus. Jesus has literally been with me every step of the way throughout this entire ordeal. He has given me renewed hope, increased my faith, comforted me, and healed all my wounds. I just want you all to know that God is good, and He will never leave us nor forsake us. Sometimes it's good to stop right where you are and give God praise at the moment for where he has brought us and where he is taking us.

After the birth of our first son, naturally, all of our focus and attention was on him. We did not make the necessary adjustments as husband and wife to reconnect together. There were a lot of inconsistencies, and the majority of time was spent raising our kids and working our jobs. We settled into a routine that made the marriage get stale at times. With me working days and my wife working nights, the disconnection was there, and it was just a lot of openings for things to go wrong in our marriage. The issues that happened earlier in our marriage didn't help matters because I was still healing and trying to get to a place where I truly forgave my wife.

I will admit I wanted her to know and feel my anger towards her. Showing her too much love and compassion too soon may have given her the idea I was completely over how she treated me. I repeatedly told her that I forgave her, but sometimes my actions did not show forgiveness. My actions displayed resentment, hurt, and disappointment. Just because I was willing to forgive her didn't mean the way I treated her would be perfect. Once I made up my mind to forgive her and decide to move forward in my marriage,

I couldn't hold her mistakes over her head forever. Repeatedly throwing sins in someone's face is not healthy for the individual or the relationship. It's a constant reminder of how they messed up, and nobody wants to hear that consistently. The word of God tells us in Ephesians 4:32 (NIV), "Be kind and compassionate to one another, forgiving each other, just as in Christ GOD forgave you." Imagine if GOD held our sins against us and constantly reminded us of all the mistakes we've made in the past. Imagine the impact that would have on our relationship with Him.

Sometimes we may feel like others don't deserve our forgiveness because of what they've said or done. We may feel justified in withholding forgiveness from them, but in reality, we're only storing up more anger, bitterness, and sadness for ourselves. Forgiving others actually gives us the freedom to move forward from our pain. I let my emotions and feelings get the best of me, and when an old friend reached out to me, I didn't shut it down like I should have. I entertained her regularly with conversations on the phone and text messages. Even though nothing sexual ever took place, emotional infidelity is real. It can be just as damaging as physical infidelity. I did not feel remorseful or guilty for talking to my friend every now and then, even though, deep down, I knew it was wrong. The emotional and mental toll of her infidelities weighed on me, so as a man, it felt good to be desired and appreciated. However, two wrongs don't make a right, and just because I was willing to forgive her didn't mean she had to forgive me.

CHAPTER EIGHT

Letting Go

*"Forget the former things;
do not dwell on the past. See,
I am doing a new thing!"
Isaiah 43:18-19 (NIV)*

When she was hurting, she hurt me, and now I was hurt and would end up hurting her. The cycle just continues to perpetuate itself until true healing has taken place. True healing can only come from God; we can talk to as many friends, family members, and therapists as possible, but true healing comes from our Savior. He can heal us in our innermost parts, where nothing or nobody else can heal us. We have a very real enemy, but it's not the people who hurt us. Our enemy will do whatever he can to drag us back into our pain and cause destruction in our lives. Even after we forgive each other, we have to stay diligent in our efforts. Forgiveness is something I had to show daily.

She did not deserve how I was treating her regardless of how she treated me. She was asking for things from me that I consistently could not give her at the moment. It was not that I didn't want to do it for her; sometimes, the mental space I was in from time to time, I couldn't bring myself to that place. *How long would it take for me to trust my wife with my heart again?* I'm the type of man who will trust you until you give me a reason not to. Once the trust has been broken, it can take a long time for it to be re-established.

In order to overcome those conflicts, I had to put on the full armor of God every day and combat the enemy's schemes by forgiving my wife as Christ first forgave me. Ephesians 6:13 (NIV) tells us to "Therefore put on the full armor of God, so that when the day of evil comes, you may be able to stand your ground, and after you have done everything, to stand." The full armor of God consists of the belt of truth buckled around your waist, the breastplate of righteousness, feet fitted with the readiness that comes from the gospel of peace, the shield of faith, the helmet of salvation and the sword of the Spirit, which is the word of God. When you go through a war, you have to be prepared to battle every day, but it's also important to remember that you may take a few hits every now and then when you are in a war. But our God is faithful, and He promised, "When you pass through the waters, I will be with you; and when you pass through the rivers, they will not sweep over you. When you walk through the fire, you will not be burned; the flames will not set you ablaze." Isaiah 43:2 (NIV). I believe that whatever we go through in life, we can learn from it and do things differently in the future.

There were some rocky times in our relationship, with good and bad moments. Every relationship faces challenges, but we have to be willing to know what our limits are and what we are willing to put up with. Everything in our relationship was not bad, and we took the great moments and tried to build on them. Having a successful marriage takes a lot of work. We were two imperfect people trying to build a solid marriage and grow together as one. It makes it more difficult when one person is trying to grow more than the other, which was the case for most of our marriage. At times it felt like she really didn't want to be married anymore. She would make comments like, "I don't think I'm marriage material" or "I don't know if I'm cut out to be a wife." She was extremely selfish; as long as she got her way, everything else would be damned, and it didn't matter. I saw all the signs of her selfishness, but I was such a man of faith I believed God could turn our marriage around and work on our hearts to be in the right place.

The truth is her heart was not into this marriage and probably had not been for a long time.

Her comments were a sign that she didn't want to be married anymore. Once an individual gets to a place where they don't want to fight for the marriage anymore, acceptance begins to set in. I slowly realized that our marriage would soon be over, and it was out of my control. In reality, there were things I could have done in the marriage, but I don't know if it would've made a difference because deep down. It's difficult to show love to someone and for that person to accept it when they don't even love things about themselves. She always had a hard time letting go of her past which would plague our marriage until the very end.

What do I do as a husband when I want to be obedient to God, but I know she is not giving me what I need in the marriage. Do I have faith in God and believe everything will get better? Of course, that is what I did, but just because I was obedient did not mean this marriage would work in my favor. I truly believe God was using me for a higher purpose to show her the unconditional love that he has for her. The book of Hosea illustrates that no one is beyond the offer of our forgiveness because no one sits outside God's offer of forgiveness. Indeed, God brings judgment on those who turn from Him. Still, Hosea's powerful act of restoration within His own marriage set the bar high for those seeking godliness in our lives. The book of Hosea provides an example of God's Love to people who have left God behind, but it also shows us what forgiveness and restoration look like in a close relationship. God intentionally had a man marry a woman who would commit adultery against him to show His Love towards her and take him to a higher level. Walking in a relationship with God will cost you something, and he will have you doing things you never imagined, but it all works out in the end.

She was so deep in her flesh and disconnected from God she couldn't receive the love I was trying to show her. After a while, when there was so much inconsistency from both of us, I got tired and wanted to give up, but I refused to accept we had come this far just to give up; we had overcome so much. We didn't exhaust all options to save our marriage, and I felt like she gave up too quickly and easily. I don't believe she felt the same way but was afraid to communicate how she was really feeling. I could tell by her actions she had checked out mentally on this marriage.

She believed getting out of this marriage would give her the freedom she was looking for. She just wanted to be free and not have to answer to anybody and just do her own thing. She was already free, so this statement had a lot of spiritual connotations behind it. She no longer had to deal with the guilt and shame of her actions or deal with my reactions to her efforts by leaving this marriage.

When I discovered she was cheating again, I was not surprised, and I honestly didn't even react the same as I did earlier in our marriage. I was disappointed for sure, but the level of pain was not the same. After being unfaithful so many times, I feel these were conscious decisions on her part. I could no longer view these as mistakes. At this point, I knew in my heart I was over this marriage, and I deserved better. I don't know if she ever stopped being unfaithful in our marriage. She honestly could have been cheating the entire time, but I will never know. What hurt me the most was her cheating on me while I was going through some medical issues. She was aware of my medical problems because we had discussions about them often. As my wife, I would've thought she would stick by my side and try to lift me up. She did a terrible job of showing that she cared about me and my health. When I was going through one of the scariest moments of my life, she didn't have my back like a spouse is supposed to.

The timing of the betrayal was just as worse than the betrayal itself. The selfishness and lack of empathy she displayed were soul-crushing. Not one time did she pray for me during this ordeal. I was extremely hurt and disappointed about that. She didn't honor any of the vows we made to each other. I realize now she wasn't in the right space spiritually to do any of this for me. For the first time in my marriage, I finally accepted and realized that this marriage should be over. I thought there was no way God would want me to suffer and stay in an unhealthy relationship like this.

Moving Forward

CHAPTER NINE

"Let your eyes look straight ahead; fix your gaze directly before you. Give careful thought to the paths for your feet and be steadfast in all your ways."
Proverbs 4:25-26 (NIV)

I would often ask God what I was supposed to be learning from everything that happened and work all this out for my good in the long run so that he would receive all the glory. I honestly had more good days than bad days throughout my marriage. I thank God for that because I know a lot of men who would have done things differently than me. I asked God, *Why tell me to marry her if all of this would happen?* The Lord revealed some important things about myself and this marriage through fasting and prayer.

One of the first things the Lord revealed to me was that I needed to be stretched to grow spiritually. There is no growth without going through trials in life. How will I ever know what I am made of and what I can handle if adversity never comes into my life? I truly learned the meaning of the scripture, *"My grace is sufficient for you, for My strength is made perfect in weakness." 2 Corinthians 12:9 (NKJV).* When I was in my weakness, the strength of the Lord was revealed to me. I had the chance to feel up close and personal how His strength was able to carry me through. My weaknesses were brought to the light throughout this ordeal, and it humbled me, but it also helped me to grow. He also revealed I have the gift of faith, which is why I was willing to forgive her and continue to love her regardless of how badly she hurt me. I trust God for the impossible, and I believe in him even when my circumstances are terrible. I know all things are possible with God, so I continued in this marriage, believing God would turn things around. I was intentional about praying for her, which revealed that, at my core, I am an intercessor. I was willing to stand in the gap and pray for her and carry her burdens when she wouldn't even do it for herself. I prayed she wouldn't hit rock bottom before turning her life around. It was like God was using me to show how he feels about His people. Even when we turn our backs on God and sin against Him, He still loves us unconditionally. I always had this overwhelming feeling of love, forgiveness, and compassion for her. My love and forgiveness towards her were a representation of how much Jesus loves her as well. Jesus loves her way more than I do, and she had a hard time receiving His Love.

The Lord also revealed to me that when she was unfaithful towards me, she was unfaithful towards Him first. He desired to be her first love, but she rejected him too. If she couldn't accept the Love of Christ, she wouldn't be able to accept mine either. As a man of God, I had to represent Christ in all that I did on a daily basis. He needed me to be an example of His Love. Although I fell short of His glory and expectations, my heart was always in the right place. The ultimate goal was for her to be restored in her relationship with Christ. No matter what we do, God still loves us, and nothing can separate us from the Love of God. That stands true for the person who is walking with the Lord and the person who is not walking with Him.

Once I finally heard from the Lord, my heart was at complete peace moving forward. The Lord had released me from this marriage, my work was done, and there was nothing else I could do. When I think about what God has meant to me during my marriage, it brings me great joy. God has been so faithful and been with me every step of the way. He has seen me through every trial and tribulation. He had shown me grace and mercy to endure when I didn't think I would make it. I know nothing but blessings will come out of everything I have endured because I have sought the Lord and been faithful with all my strength. Isaiah 61:3 tells us, "He will give a crown of beauty for ashes, a joyous blessing instead of mourning, festive praise instead of despair. In their righteousness, they will be like great oaks that the Lord has planted for His own glory." God has lifted me up and made me stronger through some of the worst experiences of my life. I learned I could press my way forward, and the circumstances of adultery would not destroy me. God can take our worst situations in life and use them for his plans and purposes to still prevail. He can get the glory out of any situation, no matter how bad it is. I understand that God has equipped me to handle this, and I thank him for giving me the endurance to make it. My spiritual increase in love, forgiveness, peace and faithfulness have been outstanding. God has done major work on my heart, and I thank him for the man I have become.

God has blessed me with many roles, and just because my marriage is over does not mean my responsibilities end with it. I am still a dad, and God has given me responsibility for my children for a reason. My kids are my top priority and making sure they are provided for, safe, and secure moving forward is essential. For my daughter, who came into my life when she was 3 years old, it is a joy and pleasure to be a father figure in her life and watch her grow into a mature young lady. She has added so much to my life, and I thank God for giving me a part of the responsibility to pour into her life. The covenant God has ordained for me to be a part of her life will never be broken. I take great pride in helping her grow spiritually and developing her relationship with the Lord.

I have two sons who will carry on the Reid namesake and legacy. God has things planned for this family for generations to come, and nothing or nobody will stop God's plans. How my sons carry themselves as Godly men, how they treat women, how they view marriage, and how they raise their own kids is part of the legacy. We still need to co-parent, so it's not just about us; It is bigger than us. The example we set for our kids will be critical. It is imperative that we continue to raise our children in the way of the Lord. No matter what happened during our marriage, I still need to respect her as the mother of my children. How I behave and speak towards my children's mother is important. They should never see or hear me disrespecting their mother. I set an example for my sons on how a man should treat a woman.

Even though this marriage didn't turn out the way I expected it to, I still believe in marriage. I haven't given up on the idea of having a wife and building my family, adding to the Reid legacy. I still believe in love and haven't given up on opening my heart to someone again. I know that God has ordained marriage, and it represents our relationship with Christ. Ephesians 5:25 (NIV) tells us, "Husbands, love your wives, just as Christ loved the church and gave himself up for her." If I want to grow as a husband, I need to fully grasp and live out this scripture. This means loving my wife unconditionally, putting her needs before my own, being selfless, wanting what is best for her, not being complacent, pursuing and desiring her, and continually lifting her up. I need to have the mindset of wanting to be a good husband. I truly believe this was my mindset when I went into my marriage. The Lord knows my heart, and my desire is to be a good husband and father. So I must believe that the Lord will reward my obedience and restore everything that has been lost or stolen from me. My ex is not the woman for me, but I know God will send the right woman my way. It's always important to remember that God is faithful in His promises. His purpose will always come to pass in our lives if we just trust in him.

When one door closes, God will open another one. Sometimes God will close a door that we want to keep open for our own good. He knows what is best for us at all times, so I trust in His plan for my life. There was purpose in my pain, and I look forward to what God has in store for my future on this journey.

About the Author

Dominic C. Reid was born and raised in Albion, MI, where he received his high school diploma from Albion Senior High. As a student-athlete, he was accepted into Albion College. While attending  Albion, Dominic received the inspiration to work with young people. He felt a sense of responsibility to his community to give back and help youth strive for a greater purpose.

After graduating from Albion, Dominic began working at Starr Commonwealth. He worked as a youth specialist and a family service counselor during his five years at Starr. While working at Starr, Dominic enrolled in graduate school at Western Michigan University to pursue his career goal of becoming a counselor. Since graduating from Western Michigan, Dominic has been a school counselor at De La Salle Collegiate and currently at Clintondale Middle School. Dominic continues to serve the youth as a mentor and track and field coach. He has a passion and belief in young people and wants them to reach their full potential. Dominic enjoys traveling, watching sports, exercising, reading, and playing video games in his free time.

Thank you for reading my story. Please consider leaving an Amazon review.

Contact information:

Facebook: Dominic Reid

Instagram: the_real_dominic_reid

Website: www.therealdominicreid.com

www.ingramcontent.com/pod-product-compliance
Lightning Source LLC
Chambersburg PA
CBHW030912080526
44589CB00010B/261